SPECTRUM®
READERS

COOL!
Sea Life

By Katharine Kenah

Carson-Dellosa
Publishing

An imprint of Carson-Dellosa Publishing, LLC
P.O. Box 35665
Greensboro, NC 27425-5665

carsondellosa.com

Printed in the USA. All rights reserved.
ISBN 978-1-62399-136-4

02-090131120

The sun is warm.
The water is blue.
People swim at the top
of the sea.
Creatures of the deep
swim below.

Manatee

A manatee is called a *sea cow*. It moves slowly in the water and eats plants.

Humpback Whale

A humpback whale has a fin on its back.
It uses its strong tail to swim.

Great White Shark

A great white shark is big
and strong.
It has lots of sharp teeth.

Crab

A crab has a hard shell.
It has eight legs and
two claws.

Sea Horse

Hammerhead Shark

A hammerhead shark has eyes
on the sides of its head.
It finds food that is far away.

Eel

An eel hides in
a hole underwater.
It waits for a fish
to eat.

Sand Dollar

A sand dollar is
as big as a cookie.
It moves and digs
in the sand.

Octopus

An octopus has three hearts and eight arms.
It uses its arms to find food.

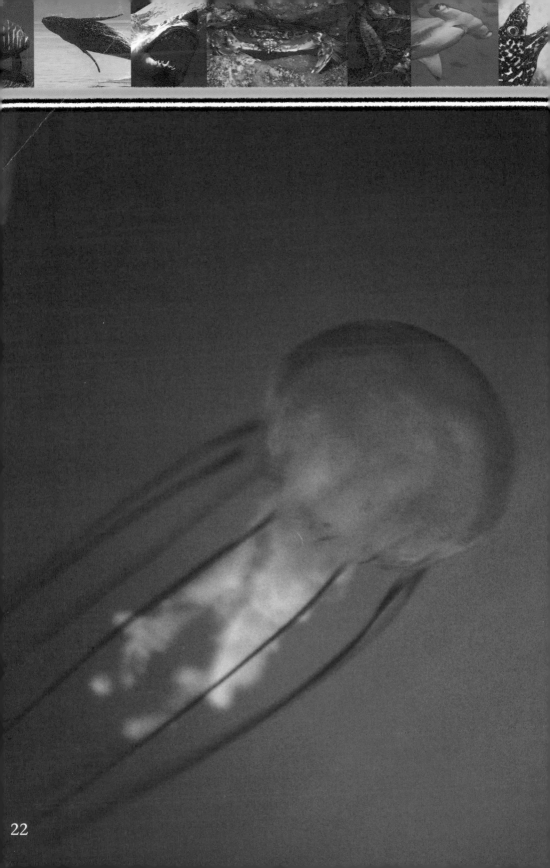

Jellyfish

A jellyfish has a soft body.
It can sting fish that
swim nearby.

Sponge

A sponge looks like a plant,
but it is an animal.
It has no head!

Dolphin

A dolphin is a small whale.
It swims and dives
in the water.

Sea Lion

A sea lion is a seal with ears.
It swims in the water and
rests on rocks.